To Her,
With Every Word

P A Gouri Sankar

ISBN

Hardcase 979-8-89632-979-4
Paperback 979-8-89610-395-0

Dedicated to
my celestial lovers, whose love writes the stars.

CONTENTS

ACKNOWLEDGMENT

First and foremost, my heartfelt gratitude goes to the unseen force that has been my constant guide. Your grace turned confusion into clarity and doubt into resolve, lighting the way when the path seemed unclear. Without your blessings, this journey would have been much harder, and for that, I am deeply humbled.

I owe an enormous thank you to my Appa, my steady guide. His regular check-ins were both a gentle nudge and a constant reminder to keep going. With patience, encouragement, and quiet optimism, he helped bring this book to life sooner than I could have hoped. And to my Amma, my creative compass—you shaped the vision behind each illustration, guiding me in choosing the art that best fit each poem. Your thoughtful ideas and insight gave this book its unique polish, ensuring that every poem and image connected with purpose.

To my sister, Rani, who walked beside me through every draft, every edit—thank you for your tireless dedication as my unofficial editor, proofreader, and trusted advisor. Without you, this collection would have been more chaos than creation.

A special mention goes to MK Uncle, who was my quiet supporter and resource gatherer, always making things fall into place when I needed them the most. And to Dr. Minu Susan Koshy Ma'am, your sharp eye and attention to detail kept the poems true to their essence. Your input was invaluable.

Finally, to everyone who played a role—my cover designers, publishers, and above all, you, the readers—thank you. Your support breathes life into these pages.

I hope these poems touch your heart, reviving memories that bring a smile to your face as we relive them together, one page at a time.

P.A.Gouri Sankar

TO HER,

It was always "her." Without her, this book would not exist. Though I choose to keep her name unspoken—for some treasures are meant to be held close—the experiences I shared are now yours to explore. Through these poems, I invite you to step into my world, to feel the emotions that once filled my heart. Perhaps as you read, you'll forget to ask her name and become an admirer—a silent, one-sided lover— just like me.

I believe that everyone, regardless of age or background, has had a "her" or "him" who brought a fresh breath of air into their lives, knowingly or unknowingly. Someone who ignited a spark, stirred the soul, and left an indelible mark on the heart. These poems are a reflection of that universal experience—a mosaic of moments filled with joy, longing, and introspection.

There are countless words I wish to say, yet "thank you" lingers first in my heart. Thank you to the moments when I sat in silence, lost without direction, and to the cherished times around her that lifted me higher than I thought possible. She was the muse, the heartbeat of every line, and within each verse, a part of her resides. She holds the missing piece of every poem, and when she reads them—if she ever does—those pieces will fall into place, breathing life into the words.

This "she" could be anyone you've loved, lost, or even once misunderstood. By the final page, I hope all that remains is a deep, tender longing—a desire to embrace them just one more time. May these words help you reconnect with those precious memories and perhaps find solace in shared experiences.

With every word, I share a piece of my soul, hoping to touch yours. This book is my tribute to her and to all the "hers" and "hims" who have inspired us, changed us, and become an unforgettable part of our stories.

PROLOGUE

Have you ever stood at the edge of a memory, where time fades and your heart builds its own world? This collection invites you into that space—one-sided love, replayed in moments that never happened but feel deeply real. Each poem is a step into the quiet dance of love, longing, and endless "what-ifs."

These poems are about her—a memory I keep returning to, a fleeting grace I can't let go. In my mind, she's still here—her laughter, her silence, her presence, all captured in these lines.

As you read, I hope you'll see love as I do—timeless, untouched by the limits of reality. These words might stir memories of your own, whether from the past or something yet to come.

Love, longing, nostalgia, and a hint of sorrow fill these pages, but they're not meant to bring sadness. Instead, they reflect hope—the kind that draws you back to old moments and dreams of what might have been.

I won't complicate it. This is simple love—unspoken, yet always there. Each poem is stitched together by the feeling of first love: the thrill, the wonder, and the worlds we create in our minds when reality feels too far away.

So, take a moment. Let this be your journey too. Nostalgia is coming.

FIRST TIME

The time has come,
To finally meet her,
It might be the first,
Or maybe the last.

A moment of magic,
Nerve-wracking too,
This feeling shall pass,
Yet I want to say, "Yes," too.

I'll wander around,
Make sure she never sees,
The fluttering soul within,
The butterflies, never at ease.

An observer of nature,
I watch them flutter,
A sweet, nervous dance,
Like caramel and butter.

LOOK AROUND

There was a time,
When fear held me tight,
But now around her,
I feel secure, just right.

Tiny stolen glances,
We met them somewhere,
No way she just saw me,
In moments so rare.

Our eyes had met,
In my silent despair,
That brief interaction,
Began our story there.

GRAZING TOUCH

She walked by,
Her hand reached out,
To take my book,
While I hid my doubt.

The courage I found,
Felt frozen in time,
No words were spoken,
Just her touch, so fine.

And then it occurred,
I gave her the book,
Her fingers brushed mine,
In that fleeting look.

To her, just a moment,
To me, it was fate,
Stuck in that second,
As she walked by straight.

THE TALK

A shot of espresso,
After an all-nighter's grind,
Her words so electric,
They jolt my mind,
Pulling me back,
From any daydream I find.

A breeze of cool air,
On a hot summer's sway,
Invisible yet stirring,
In its gentle display,
Just like her voice,
I could listen all day.

CALLS UNCUT

Holding hands was my second love,
The first, getting lost
In the brown dunes of her eyes,
Falling into their whirlpool,
A desert oasis in disguise.

Close up to stay awake,
Calls that ran all night,
Sleepless hours,
Lines never cut,
I often wonder,
Who said goodbye first in that quiet hush?

The hours with her,
Turn minutes uncounted,
Gone in a heartbeat,
Or a flash of thunder,
The night breaks into day,
As she whispers, "Let me see you today."

LOOK AWAY

Stealing glances secretly,
No moment to waste,
Every second counted,
In this quiet chase.

FALL AGAIN

I'd impress you,
With all the flowers in bloom,
Maybe that would suffice.

But wait,
A bittersweet pause,
Your smile so bright,
Might cause a petal to fall,
And make me fall for you twice.

HER CHARM

Someone once said, "Character is beauty,"
I confirmed the latter,
The moment I saw you,
For the first time.

The former proved true as well,
When you asked, "Are you okay?"
And gently made me say,
"I'm not alright, can you help me too?"
And you smiled and said,
"Come, let me talk to you."

WOBBLING HEART

The wobble in my walk,
As my friends pointed out,
Was all because of her,
they said,
I shrugged off their doubt.
Maybe yes,
Or maybe no,
I'll take the blame,
For my heart's glow.

SWING BY

It was the thrill
Of just being near,
That made me flutter
Without wings, yet clear,
Stirring my stomach
Like a swing in the air,
Best to stay away,
Or be swept in her flair.

RIPPLES ON THE CLOCK

The ripples on water,
Oscillate and sway,
They come and they go,
Like a clock ticking away.
I wish the time with you,
Could ripple like a clock,
Flowing back and forth,
In a mesmerising lock.

The ripples may fade,
By nature's own hand,
But my time with you,
Will forever withstand.
For while ripples subside,
In nature's embrace,
You are my world,
In every time and space.

ALLURING AURA

The smell of the earth
After the rain's fall,
The scent of flowers,
By the temple wall,
All remind me
Of your glowing aura,
My senses awake,
Like the bright aurora.

WEIGHTLESS WAVES

Eternity seemed far,
Yet I could feel it near,
Oh! It was as close as,
You standing here.
You, my eternity,
In the weightless waves,
Of your flowing hair,
That endlessly sways.
As I run my fingers through,
Lost in the sea of you,
You become infinity,
In all I do.

COFFEE TABLE

The warm exchanges,
We shared that day,
In the coffee shop,
Still feel fresh in a way.
You laughed aloud,
While I admired in silence,
Caught up in the moment,
Without any defiance.

Now, as I pass by the shop,
With coffee in the air,
The only thing that lingers,
Is the memory we shared there.
Our words come rushing back,
And the coffee's embrace,
Still lingering on my mind,
A taste time won't erase.

HUES FALL

It's in the eyes,
It's in the eyes,
They always say,
And the only way
I could be sure,
Was to drown in their hue,
Though everyone warned me,
Not to fall through.

PASSING CLOUDS

Out of all the passing clouds,
One caught my gaze,
It moved with grace,
In soft, gentle ways.

It held the warmth
Of a tight embrace,
And a heartfelt touch,
That I could trace.

I saw you there,
I felt you near,
There's nothing I want,
But to keep you here.

Just pure love,
No space, no fuss,
You are my sky,
My only nimbus.

FOUND YOU!

We were playing hide and seek,
And I was the one who'd chase,
She was a keeper, a perfect hider,
Vanishing without a trace.
It seemed so hard to find her,
But I wasn't alone in the game.

Then out of nowhere, someone flew,
As if summoned by the breeze,
A tiny guest who found her first,
With effortless ease.

It was the butterfly,
Her flower it had claimed,
It found its peace, pure and sweet,
In this game, I faced defeat.

SYNC IN TIME

Sometimes,
I just want to be understood,
Like you turning to the page,
Where my bookmark stood.
Like you glancing at the clock,
At the same time I do,
Like sending a message,
And your reply pings through.

Our words collide,
In a perfect rhyme,
Like we're connected,
By the same line of time.
And just holding hands,
Without a word to share,
In the quiet stillness,
As we both silently stare.
When you, too, want to be understood,
Right there.

SPARROW IN THE WIND

Taking small steps closer to you,
One step at a time,
Like the sparrow inching,
Toward its seeds in line.
But at the faintest sound,
Of dry leaves in the breeze,
It takes flight in fear,
As if chased by the trees.

Just like that,
When I try to come near,
To feel your presence,
And hold you dear,
The moment you notice,
I'm standing so close,
My soul leaps away,
To a world it knows.

WINTER WISH

Sometimes I wished,
Winter would stay a bit longer,
For I cherished those nights,
When our bond felt stronger,
Walking through the park,
With no one else in sight,
Just you and me,
In the quiet moonlight.

Plowing through the snow,
One step at a time,
Talking as fog rose,
From breaths so sublime,
We'd laugh and smile,
Through shivering teeth,
As we stood together,
On the ice beneath.

Now that summer's here,
There's no turning back,
But I long to trace,
Our footsteps on that track.
If I had stayed a bit longer,
I still sit and wonder,
And wish again,
That winter stayed longer.

HUMBLE THOUGHTS

In all my unrequited dreams,
I still find you near,
I try to mend what wasn't broken,
At least, not from here.
I strive to stay the humble one,
Though far from right, I stand,
But I hold on, despite the distance,
Reaching for your hand.

The idea was never clear,
Deception not the game,
I knew from the start,
Yet tried all the same.
What more can I do,
But linger close around,
Staying present and seen,
Hoping to be found.

CHASING SECRETS

I trust these pages,
More than anyone around,
For I know they'll keep,
My feelings safe and sound.
They won't betray my heart,
At the wrong time or place,
Or spill my secret thoughts,
To the one I still chase.

FAREWELL UNSEEN

The end of the line,
Don't you think it's a bit overstated?
It lifts you high,
For something once celebrated,
That never existed in real time,
Until I watched her leave,
Leaving me where she found me,
In a moment I couldn't believe.

Her glance pulled me in,
And hit me like a trance,
A silent test she gave,
Without a single chance.
The paper she handed,
Blank, with nothing to say,
Perhaps it was permission,
Or a request to walk away.

Or maybe a quiet message,
That she was fading fast,
To her, I'd become a ghost,
A shadow of the past.
I crave her still,
Though my heart protests,
For now, my life's become
A bitter detest.

MEMORIES ALONE

I thought you were the solution,
A solace to my peace,
To quiet the restless thoughts,
And let the chaos cease.
I believed I could be calm,
Or let my mind find ease,
But still, I seek your glimpse,
In moments such as these.

The thoughts I hold so dear,
Still linger in my mind,
If left to fade away,
They'd rot and fall behind.
Settled in my mind,
Restless as we speak,
I still pursue the memory,
Of you I cannot reach.

DAY DREAMS

Dreams have been rough these days,
Daydreams haunt me too,
It's not the usual nightmares creeping in,
But the fear of losing you.
No demons rise to terrify,
No shadows take the blame,
It's the thought of you slipping away,
That shakes me all the same.

INNER SOUL

Look at her,
Isn't she divine?
She is—no doubt,
With beauty that shines.
That's what everyone said,
Admiring her grace,
But it was all surface,
No depth to embrace.

I was no different,
Captivated by her glance,
But to know her soul,
I never stood a chance.
Busy as she was,
Far beyond my league,
A fleeting moment,
In a silent intrigue.

HIS OPINION

Not again,
Oh, God, no!
Why is she the one
My mind won't let go?
There are many more,
But it's her I see,
I try to erase,
Her memories from me.

I've crossed them out,
Every thought, every part,
But still, I wonder,
Does she know my heart?
God whispered, "She doesn't see
What you hold so deep.
Maybe it's a secret
Only your heart can keep."

EPILOGUE

A decade ago, I found myself scribbling verses in the margins of old notebooks, capturing feelings I couldn't express aloud. Back then, I never imagined these scattered thoughts would one day form a collection, let alone find their way into your hands. When I revisited those notebooks, I realized that these words weren't meant to be hidden—they were meant to be shared. My hope in doing so was simple: to show that silent, unspoken love is real, deeply felt by people like you and me.

Returning to these poems has felt like reconnecting with a younger version of myself. Though time has passed and life has changed, the emotions captured in these lines remain as true as they were when I first wrote them. Now that you've read through this collection, I hope that honesty has come through to you. Knowing these words have resonated with someone else is a dream realized, and I am profoundly grateful.

Perhaps you've experienced a range of emotions—maybe the quiet ache of unspoken love, the bittersweet pull of nostalgia, or the lingering hope for what might have been. These were my feelings then, and perhaps they've mirrored some of your own.

Writing has always been a way for me to process emotions that words often struggle to capture. Each poem is a snapshot, allowing me to revisit the past and see it in a clearer light. Through this journey, I've come to understand how love, in all its forms, quietly shapes who we become.

As you close this book, I hope it leaves you with a gentle sense of reflection. Perhaps these poems have stirred feelings, new or old, or reminded you of experiences that linger just beneath the surface. In that, know that you're not alone.

Thank you for sharing this journey with me. May these poems have touched your heart, sparked a memory, or perhaps even encouraged you to embrace the quiet strength of unspoken love in your life.

And should you ever feel inclined to share your thoughts, reflections, or even suggestions for making this collection better, I would be honoured to hear from you. Each message will be cherished and thoughtfully answered. You can reach me at ***pagourisankarauthor@gmail.com***—your words are welcome here

ABOUT THE AUTHOR

P A Gouri Sankar spends his days navigating the corporate world, but when work ends, his true passion takes over—writing poetry. Based in Chennai, he has mastered the balance between professional life and his love for words, transforming everyday moments into verses that resonate deeply.

A keen observer of life, Gouri Sankar draws inspiration from the subtle details and simple experiences that often go unnoticed. He believes that the most profound emotions are found in life's quietest moments, and he captures them with sincerity and grace.

This collection of poems reflects his journey—profound, heartfelt, and relatable to anyone who has ever loved silently or cherished a fleeting moment. Through his poetry, he invites readers to pause, reflect, and find beauty in the everyday nuances of life.

All images in this book are AI-generated.
All the illustrations are done by Aaron Gauskaip.